Stories
of
GREAT PEOPLE

Armstrong's moon rock

Gerry Bailey and Karen Foster

**Illustrated by Leighton Noyes
and Karen Radford**

♣ **Crabtree Publishing Company**
www.crabtreebooks.com

S0-ARO-035

Mr. RUMMAGE has a stall piled high with interesting objects—and he has a great story to tell about each and every one of his treasures.

DIGBY PLATT is an antique collector. Every Saturday he picks up a bargain at Mr. Rummage's antique stall and loves listening to the story behind his new 'find'.

HANNAH PLATT is Digby's argumentative, older sister— and she doesn't believe a word that Mr. Rummage says!

PIXIE the market's fortuneteller sells incense, lotions and potions, candles, mandalas, and crystals inside her exotic stall.

Crabtree Publishing Company
www.crabtreebooks.com

Other books in the series

Credits

Bettmann/Corbis: 13 bottom corner, 16 corner right, 18 bottom left, 23 bottom left
Comstock/Superstock: backgrounds 17, 22, 24, 26–27
David J. & Janice L. Frent Collection/Corbis: 24 bottom left
JPL: 26 left
NASA: 9 top right, 9 bottom right, 14 bottom left, 14 top right, 17 bottom right, 18 top left, 21 top left, 21 center, 21 bottom right, 22 top left, 22 bottom, 23 top left, 24 top left, 26 top right, 27 bottom left, 28 bottom, 29 top, 29 bottom right, 33 bottom, 35
NASA-KSC: 30 bottom left, 30 top right, 33 top
Neil Rabinowitz/Corbis: 10 center

Picture research: Diana Morris info@picture-research.co.uk

Library and Archives Canada Cataloguing in Publication

Bailey, Gerry
    Armstrong's moon rock / Gerry Bailey and Karen Foster ;
illustrated by Leighton Noyes and Karen Radford.

(Stories of great people)
Includes index.
ISBN 978-0-7787-3684-4 (bound).--ISBN 978-0-7787-3706-3 (pbk.)

    1. Armstrong, Neil, 1930- --Juvenile fiction. 2. Project Apollo
(U.S.)--Juvenile fiction. 3. Space flight to the moon--Juvenile fiction.
4. Astronauts--United States--Biography--Juvenile fiction.
I. Foster, Karen, 1959- II. Noyes, Leighton III. Radford, Karen
IV. Title. V. Series.

PZ7.B15Ar 2008   j823'.92   C2007-907615-7

Library of Congress Cataloging-in-Publication Data

Bailey, Gerry.
  Armstrong's moon rock / Gerry Bailey and Karen Foster ; illustrated by
Leighton Noyes and Karen Radford.
    p. cm. -- (Stories of great people)
  Includes index.
  ISBN-13: 978-0-7787-3684-4 (rlb)
  ISBN-10: 0-7787-3684-9 (rlb)
  ISBN-13: 978-0-7787-3706-3 (pb)
  ISBN-10: 0-7787-3706-3 (pb)
  1. Armstrong, Neil, 1930- --Juvenile literature. 2. Astronauts--United States--
Biography--Juvenile literature. 3. Project Apollo (U.S.)--Juvenile literature. 4.
Space flight to the moon--Juvenile literature. I. Foster, Karen, 1959- II. Noyes,
Leighton, ill. III. Radford, Karen, ill. IV. Title.
  TL789.85.A75B35 2008
  629.4092--dc22
  [B]
                       2007051247

Crabtree Publishing Company
www.crabtreebooks.com   1-800-387-7650

Published in Canada
Crabtree Publishing
616 Welland Ave.
St. Catharines, Ontario
L2M 5V6

Published in the United States
Crabtree Publishing
PMB 59051
350 Fifth Avenue, 59th Floor
New York, New York 10118

Published by CRABTREE PUBLISHING COMPANY
Copyright © **2008** Diverta Ltd.
Printed in the USA/012010/CG20091229

All rights reserved. No part of this publication may be
reproduced, stored in a retrieval system or be transmitted
in any form or by any means, electronic, mechanical,
photocopying, recording, or otherwise, without the prior
written permission of Crabtree Publishing Company.

ARMSTRONG'S MOON ROCK

Table of Contents

Every Saturday morning, Knicknack Market comes to life. The street vendors are there almost before the sun is up. And by the time you and I are out of bed, the stalls are built, the boxes are opened, and all the goods are carefully laid out on display.

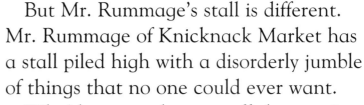

Objects are piled high. Some are laid out on velvet: precious necklaces and jeweled swords. Others stand upright at the back: large, framed pictures of very important people, lamps made from tasseled satin, and old-fashioned cash registers—the kind that jingle when the drawers are opened.

And then there are things that stay in their boxes all day, waiting for the right customer to come along: war medals laid out in straight lines, stopwatches on leather straps, and utensils in polished silver for all those special occasions.

But Mr. Rummage's stall is different. Mr. Rummage of Knicknack Market has a stall piled high with a disorderly jumble of things that no one could ever want.

Who'd want to buy a stuffed mouse?
Or a broken umbrella?
Or a pair of false teeth?

Mr. Rummage has them all. And, as you can imagine, they don't cost a lot!

Rummage's Antiques

Digby Platt—ten year-old collector of antiques—was off to see his friend Mr. Rummage of Knicknack Market. It was Saturday and, as usual, Digby's weekly allowance was burning a hole in his pocket.

But Digby wasn't going to spend it on any old thing. It had to be something rare and interesting for his collection, something from Mr. Rummage's incredible stall. Hannah, his older sister, had come along as usual. She had secret doubts about the value of Mr. Rummage's objects and felt, for some big-sisterly reason, that she had to stop her little brother from buying useless bits of junk.

"Well, look who's here—my two favorite customers." said Mr. Rummage, who was chatting with Pixie, who told fortunes at a tent down the street.

"Hello Mr. Rummage, hello Pixie," greeted the children.

"Hey, what's this?" asked Digby, pointing to a piece of rock wedged in front of a picture of an astronaut.

"Put it down, Digby!" said Hannah. "It's just an ordinary stone, silly. Don't waste your money on things like that.

I'll get rid of it," and she picked up the rock to throw it away.

"Wait!" shouted Pixie as she leapt to her feet to stop Hannah. "That's no ordinary bit of rock—it's very precious, isn't it Mr. Rummage?"

"Pixie's right," said Mr. Rummage. "That rock's come all the way from the moon—in the pocket of the astronaut, Neil Armstrong."

NEIL ARMSTRONG

Neil Alden Armstrong was born on August 5, 1930 in Wapakoneta, Ohio. His parents were Stephen and Viola Armstrong. Neil was actually born on his grandparents' farm. His father was a public official for the State of Ohio, and the family moved around a lot. They lived in Warren, Jefferson, Ravenna, St. Mary's, and Upper Sandusky before finally settling in Wapakoneta. Neil's family also included his brother, Dean, and his sister, June.

Let's find out more...

HIGH FLIER

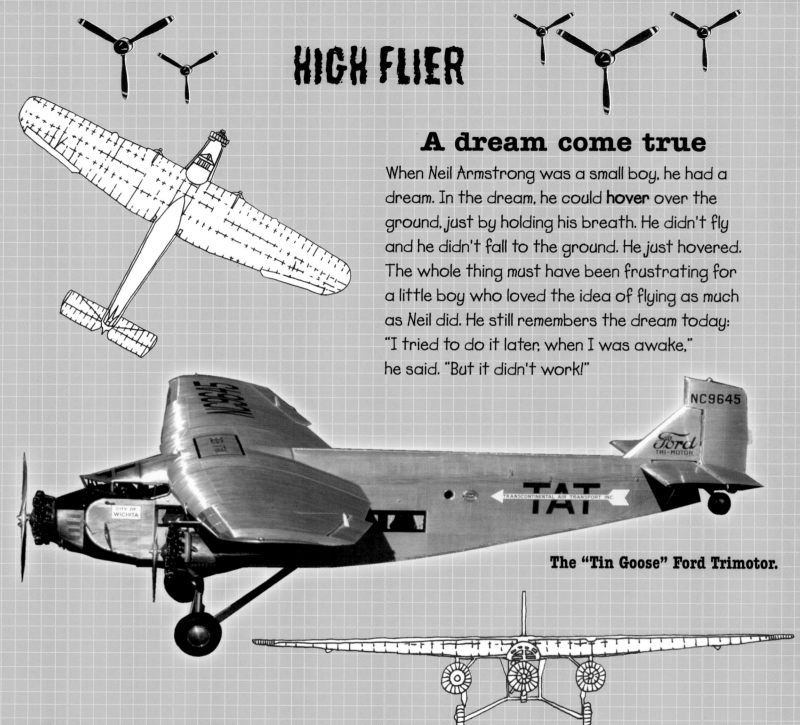

A dream come true

When Neil Armstrong was a small boy, he had a dream. In the dream, he could **hover** over the ground, just by holding his breath. He didn't fly and he didn't fall to the ground. He just hovered. The whole thing must have been frustrating for a little boy who loved the idea of flying as much as Neil did. He still remembers the dream today: "I tried to do it later, when I was awake," he said. "But it didn't work!"

The "Tin Goose" Ford Trimotor.

Ride in a "Tin Goose"

Neil's first plane ride was in a Ford Trimotor, affectionately called the "Tin Goose," It was the first passenger plane made with a metal outer skin instead of the old combination of cloth, wire, and wood. Powered by three Pratt & Whitney engines, it had a cruise speed of just 90 miles per hour. (145 km/h) which was very fast in those days.

"What! You mean THAT Neil Armstrong, the first man on the moon?" spluttered Digby. "Gosh, Mr. Rummage, can I see?"

"The very one," beamed Mr. Rummage showing Digby the rock. "The very one."

"I bet he always wanted to be an astronaut," said Digby, "I know I do."

"Yes, after you've been a train driver, parmedic, and a pilot," said Hannah, rolling her eyes.

"I never said I wanted to be…"

"Neil didn't always want to be an astronaut," interrupted Mr. Rummage. "But he loved the idea of flying."

"Like Superman?" suggested Digby.

"No," said Mr. Rummage. "Neil liked planes. He was introduced to aircraft by his father and took his first plane ride when he was just six years old."

"Wow, what kind of plane was it?" asked Digby excitedly.

"It was an old Ford Trimotor. They called it a 'Tin Goose' back in 1936."

"Sounds risky," giggled Hannah, "I'm surprised it managed to stay up in the air."

"Of course it did, what do you think propellers are for?" said Digby. "I know because I've been on a plane."

"Huh, you mean on the rides at the fair," said Hannah.

"No it wasn't," squealed Digby. "I went on a plane last year when we went on vaction. And you came too, so you know it's true."

"Well, it wasn't exactly a breakthrough in flying history," said Hannah, "and it doesn't make you into a Neil Armstrong."

"All right, you two, stop arguing," said Rummage, holding up his hands in mock exasperation. "Times are a lot different now—we're used to flying. But Digby's right. It's still an adventure."

"Anyway," Mr. Rummage went on, "from the age of nine Neil was an aircraft nut. He just loved all kinds of planes. In fact, he was obsessed."

"What's that mean?" asked Digby.

"Well, it means he didn't think of much else," replied Mr. Rummage. "As for a trip to the moon—well, he could never have guessed how things would turn out. Moon flights were still pure science fiction. And Neil was just a kid who still had a lot to learn."

"Like someone else I know," said Hannah, looking at her brother. "I suppose because he was a boy, young Neil was allowed to fly the plane," said Hannah huffily.

"No—that would have been too risky," said Mr. Rummage. "But afterward he did odd jobs around town to pay for flying lessons. He trained in an Aeronca Champion plane and got his licence on his sixteeth birthday."

"Wicked! He must have been an awsome pilot," said Digby.

"He was—good enough to join the United States Navy and get an aeronautical engineering scholarship."

"So he went from being a great pilot to being a boring engineer," scoffed Hannah.

"He didn't have a chance to get bored," said Mr. Rummage. "He was sent a few months later to fight in the Korean War."

COMBAT PILOT

Jet pilot

During the Korean War, Armstrong piloted 78 combat missions from the aircraft carrier USS Essex. He flew a Grumman F9F-2 Panther. It was one of the most stylish planes ever built. Sleek and handsome, it was the first jet fighter to be used widely by the United States Navy and the Marines. It was also the first navy jet to shoot down an enemy plane. Although it wasn't quite as good as the Russian MiG-15s, it shot down five of them. Each Panther could carry bombs and rockets.

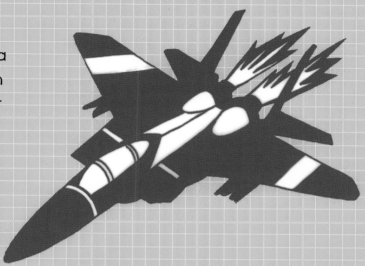

When Neil got home, he was awarded the Air Medal and two Gold Stars for his bravery.

Aeronca Champion

Aeronca, or the Aeronautical Corporation of America, was formed in 1928. It became the first company to produce a light plane that sold well, the Aeronca C2. It was called the "Flying Bathtub" because of its open body. The C2 helped promote private flying and was the first airplane to be refueled while in the air—a man in a speeding car would hand up a can of fuel that the pilot hooked with a wooden cane! Aeronca continued to develop its aircraft and in 1954 certified the Aeronca Champion. It became the most popular plane the company ever made. Neil Armstrong flew one while training to be a pilot. Luckily for him, the plane had a properly enclosed cockpit!

13

IN TRAINING

"Go fever"

Russians and Americans took the Space Race very seriously. They were almost fighting a war—not with weapons, but with spacecraft and achievements in space. The war would be "won," people felt, by the first nation to reach the final goal—a moon landing. In the United States, everyone was caught up in the excitement of the idea. NASA's Mercury and Gemini projects prepared the way for the Apollo program which would reach the moon.

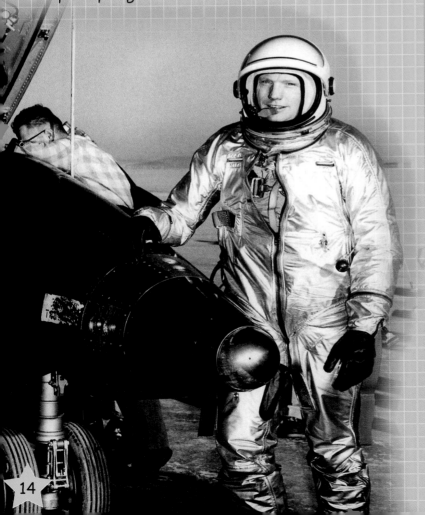

Research pilot

Neil Armstrong joined NACA—the National Advisory Committee for Aeronautics—as a research pilot at the Lewis Laboratory in Cleveland, Ohio. He then went to the NACA High Speed Flight Station at Edwards Air Force Base in California. As a project pilot, he experimented with high-speed aircraft, including the 4,000 miles per hour (6,437km/h) X-15. But he learned the ropes in a World War II P-51 Mustang. He also worked on the development of "hypersonic" flight—faster than five times the speed of sound—and flew over 200 different types of aircraft, including jets, rockets, helicopters, and gliders.

Astronaut training

Armstrong had the right nature and abilities to become an astronaut. His training with NASA included getting used to being weightless, which meant swimming around in a tank of water while wearing a space suit. He was also spun around in a gyro machine to experience the high gravitational forces he'd have to absorb at lift off. And he stuck to a strict fitness plan so he'd be strong and healthy enough for the rigors of space travel.

"I bet he was glad to get home from the war and feel safe again," said Hannah.

"Not really," shrugged Mr. Rummage, "he didn't want 'safe'—he wanted to do something exciting, and dangerous. So he became a test pilot."

"Cool!" cried Digby. "I bet he got to fly all kinds of great planes."

"He did a lot more than just fly planes, Digby. He was an engineer and a scientist—a man on the cutting edge of flight. He probably thought the space flight guys were amateurs."

"So why did he become an astronaut?" asked Hannah.

"Well, I suppose when the Apollo space program was created and a trip to the moon became a reality, Neil became convinced," said Mr. Rummage. "That was after fellow astronaut John Glenn had **orbited** Earth, of course."

"I know someone who I would like to send into space," said Hannah, looking at Digby.

"At least I'm smart enough to be an astronaut," he shot back at her.

"All right you two," said Mr. Rummage quietly. "Just as well you weren't competing in the Space Race. You'd have spent more time arguing than building spacecraft."

"Sorry, Mr. Rummage," said Hannah looking embarrassed. "Anyway, what was the Space Race?"

"I know," said Digby, importantly. "It was the race between Russia and America to get to space."

"Yes, but more than that, it was to see who'd be first to put a man on the moon. And that kind of challenge must have excited Neil Armstrong."

"Come in Mission Control."

"Of course, humans weren't the first space travelers," said Mr. Rummage.

"You mean aliens were out there?" said Digby, his eyes almost popping out of his head.

"No, not quite, Digby. The first space travelers were animals. Dogs, cats, chimps, a frog, and heaven knows how many others. Scientists used them first so that humans didn't have to take as many risks."

"That's not fair," said Hannah indignantly. "Who fed them? I hope that they were not allowed to starve."

"Oh no," said Mr. Rummage, "they were provided with automatic feeders and made comfortable. And because they provided so much useful information, they were considered heroes as much as the astronauts."

Muttnik

Russians used nine dogs to test space suits in unpressurized cabins of space capsules. The most famous was a stray mongrel called Laika, or "barker," in Russian. Laika was hurled into space on November 3, 1957 aboard Sputnik 2. Americans nicknamed her "Muttnik." She was the first dog to go into orbit and she showed no ill effects while she was there—nearly 2,000 miles (3,219 km) above Earth's surface.

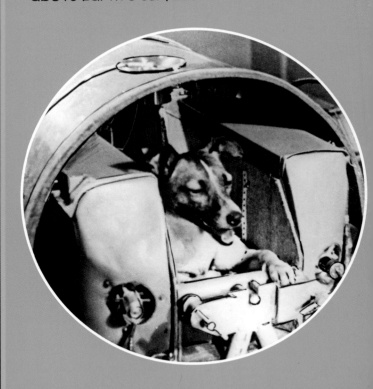

Laika could eat and drink while harnessed inside the capsule. Wires were attached to her body to transmit her heartbeat, blood pressure, and breathing rate back to **Mission Control.**

COSMIC PETS

When scientists built rockets that could take a living thing into space, they decided not to risk a human. Instead, they used animals and observed how they reacted. Would people be able to function in space, or would they become sick? No one knew, of course, because no-one had been there.

Astro-animals

They sound like characters from a science-fiction film, but there actually have been astro-frogs, spiders from space, and cosmo-ants. Felix the cat went into space, as did a chimpanzee called Ham. Both provided scientists with information on how the body reacts in space. Just what data Otolith the frog provided or Arabella the garden spider, only the scientists know.

Test mannequin

Russians also used a test **mannequin** called Ivan Ivanovich. He was so realistic that they had to stamp the word "model" on his forehead, just in case anyone found him on landing!

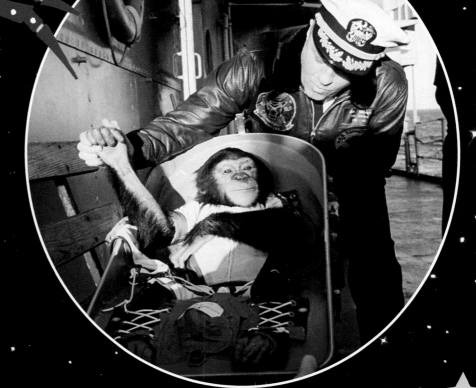

THE GEMINI PROJECT

The Gemini project of 1962 was part of America's step-by-step plan to put a man on the moon ahead of the Soviet Union—in what became known as the Space Race. Before the project began, the U.S. had spent a total of just two days and six hours in space—not nearly long enough to embark on a moon mission.

The visor of Ed White's helmet was gold-plated to keep out the sun's harmful rays.

Goals

The Gemini mission aimed to perfect the technology needed for a moon flight. This included "rendezvous" and "docking" practice (when spacecraft meet and link up in space). Other goals were spacewalking, using tools in space, and extending the amount of time astronauts spent in space. In all, 12 missions were completed in less than 20 months for $3.5 billion, while 16 new astronauts made trips into space.

The Gemini capsules were very cramped—only 19 feet (5.8 m) long and 19 feet (3 m) wide.

Achievements

- Gemini 1 and 2 were unmanned missions.
- Gemini 3 successfully launched two men into space.
- Gemini 4 saw the first American spacewalk.
- Ed White, who was connected to the craft by a lifeline, walked in space for 22 minutes.
- Neil Armstrong and Dave Scott finally made the first docking in Gemini 8.
- Mike Collins transferred to another craft on the Gemini 10 mission.
- The final flight was Gemini 12, which took astronauts James A. Lovell and Buzz Aldrin into space on November 11, 1966.

"In 1962, Neil Armstrong joined the Gemini program."

"What was that?" asked Hannah.

"Gemini was the name for a series of spacecraft named after twin stars," replied Mr. Rummage. "It was on the Gemini 8 flight that Neil proved he was good enough to be the commander of the first moon mission."

"What happened?" asked Digby.

"Well, his orders were to dock with a target vehicle that had been launched into space a few hours earlier. Despite a few computer problems, he and his partner, Dave Scott, got under way on March 16, 1966."

"Everything went according to plan, then?" speculated Hannah.

"Well, it did until the two craft were linked together. But then they began to spin out of control. Neil knew he had to do something fast—the two men were close to losing consciousness."

"Oh no!" cried Hannah, hardly able to endure the suspense.

"A few more seconds and they would have died in space. But Neil coolly decided to unlock the capsule from the target craft and fire the reentry rockets. Thirty minutes later Gemini 8 was under control again."

"Just in time," sighed Digby, "I thought they were goners."

"They weren't out of danger yet," said Mr. Rummage. "The craft was now low on fuel and out of range of the tracking stations. Even so, Neil was able to get the thing down and they splashed into the Pacific Ocean safely. The rest, as they say, is history."

"The right man for a crisis," smiled Hannah.

"Or a moon landing."

"Neil must have been really excited once he knew he was part of the moon mission," said Digby.

"He was," said Mr. Rummage. "This was the big one. It was an awesome sight when the huge Saturn rocket, with the tiny command and **lunar modules** on top, rolled out onto the launch pad at Cape Kennedy."

"Wow!" muttered Digby, trying to imagine it all.

"Meanwhile, the astronauts got suited up," said Mr. Rummage. "They looked calm as they walked across to the launching tower and climbed aboard the command module."

"They must have had to make some last-minute computer checks," said Digby.

"Yes, they made sure they could communicate with Mission Control, and soon they were seconds away from liftoff."

The children watched, wide-eyed and mouths open as Mr. Rummage began the countdown. "Three, two, one, LIFTOFF!" They screamed with excitement.

"There was a terrible shaking and rumbling as the engines ignited," he went on. "Then Saturn V rose off the launch pad, leaving a fiery trail as it rocketed skyward. The craft gathered speed and the crew were slammed back in their seats as huge forces set to work, causing them to feel four times Earth's gravity. Once the first, second, and third parts, or stages, of the rocket had done their job and dropped away, Neil and the other astronauts experienced the weird floating sensation of weightlessness. Everything had gone okay."

"Thank goodness," whispered Hannah as if lift off had happened right there and then.

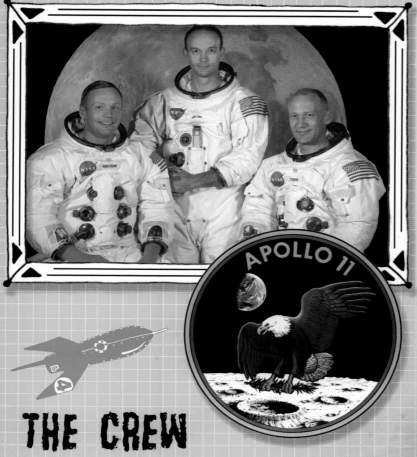

Apollo 11 liftoff

Apollo 11 was made up of three different sections: the command module, named Columbia, the service module, and the lunar landing module, named Eagle. Columbia was the crew's living quarters, while the service module contained supplies such as fuel and oxygen. The lunar module was designed to make the hazardous descent to the moon's surface and then return to Columbia. Neil Armstrong and Buzz Aldrin rode the Eagle to the moon, where they spent three days. Mike Collins stayed aboard Columbia as it orbited above the moon.

THE CREW

NEIL ARMSTRONG was commander of Apollo 11, the first manned lunar landing mission. He became the first man to land a spacecraft on the moon and to walk on its surface.

BUZZ ALDRIN graduated from West Point and then flew Sabre jets in the Korean War. He specialized in astronautics and joined NASA. Then, in 1966, he set a spacewalking record during the Gemini 12 mission. Buzz became the second man to set foot on the moon.

MIKE COLLINS also trained at West Point and then became a flight test officer at Edwards Air Force Base. He joined NASA in 1963 and piloted the Gemini 10 mission—so he was the obvious choice to pilot the Apollo 11 command module.

Satellite picture of a swirling hurricane.

CABIN WITH A VIEW

The astronauts described the amazing sights they saw from the windows of their capsule as they rose higher and higher above Earth's surface—the brown savannas of Africa, the vast turquoise-blue panorama of the Indian Ocean, the great Rocky Mountains range that stretched like a backbone down North America. Then there were the brilliant white plains of Antarctica, and the mighty Nile and Amazon rivers, winding out to sea. It was a wonderful experience.

To the moon

Soon their tiny spacecraft was hurtling toward the moon at 25,000 miles per hour (40,234 km/h). At first Earth, shrouded in swirling clouds, filled the porthole. But as they drew away it became smaller and smaller. The moon, on the other hand, grew larger as they flew towards it. At last, three days after liftoff, the Apollo astronauts were looking at the huge, dark disk that blocked out the stars and was their destination.

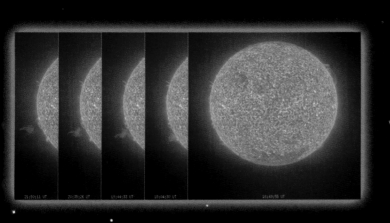

From sunrise to earthrise

Once in orbit around the moon, the crew saw their first airless sunrise. Bright streamers of light radiated huge distances from the sun, then a spike of brilliant light shot out from the moon's horizon as sunrise began. Best of all, though, was seeing the green-blue globe of the Earth loom up from the horizon in a spectacular Earthrise.

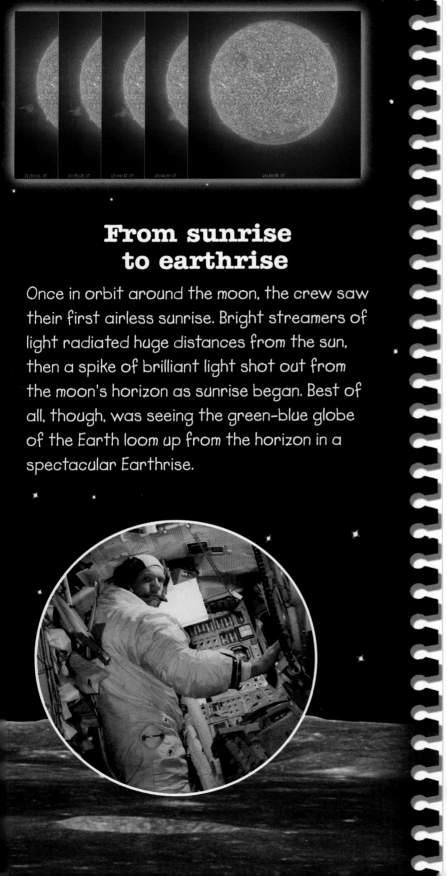

"What happened while they were in space?" asked Digby. "What did they see?"

"Well," began Mr. Rummage, "in a rocket things speed by at an alarming rate. But they would have seen wonderful views of the oceans, continents, and cloud patterns below."

"It must've been just like looking at a map,' said Hannah.

"Partly," said Mr. Rummage, "except this was real—especially the twinkling lights of the cities, and the flashes of lightning darting from black clouds over the South Pacific. You wouldn't see that on a map."

MOONWALK

Television Show

July 18th 1969, the crew began a 96-minute color-TV transmission of the command module and the lunar module interiors. People watching were fascinated to see them floating about in the cabin, weightless. Viewers also got to see the outside of the command module. the moon's surface, pictures of Earth from space, and the spacecraft tunnel hatch opening.

Buzz Aldrin on the moon during the Apollo 11 mission.

Giant leaps

When Neil Armstrong stepped onto the moon, he and his equipment weighed around 60 lb (27 kg). On Earth they would have weighed over 350 lb (60 kg) That's because the pull of gravity on the Moon is less than it is on Earth. So Armstrong and Aldrin were able to take "giant leaps," even with heavy space suits on.

APOLLO 11 ASTRONAUTS
Michael Collins
Command Module Pilot
Neil A. Armstrong
Commander
Edwin E. Aldrin, Jr.
Lunar Module Pilot
SUNDAY JULY 20th 1969 – FIRST MAN ON THE MOON
NEIL A. ARMSTRONG
FIRST MEN ON THE MOON

Touchdown

At 4:17 p.m. EDT on July 20, half of the Apollo mission was accomplished. Neil Armstrong piloted the lunar module, the Eagle, to a touchdown on the moon. He had just 30 seconds worth of fuel left for the landing. Immediately, he reported to Mission Control at MSC, "Houston, Tranquillity Base here—the Eagle has landed." Six hours later at 10:56 p.m. EDT, Armstrong took the first step on the surface of the Moon.

"Armstrong's greatest achievement" said Mr. Rummage, "was the moon landing. After piloting the Eagle down to the surface, he stepped out of the craft, climbed slowly down the ladder and placed the first human foot on the moon. As his left toe touched the ground, he famously said "one small step for man—one giant leap for mankind."

"They're great words, aren't they?" said Digby.

"They certainly are,' said Mr. Rummage, "except that's not quite what he said."

"Of course it is,' said Hannah confidently, "everyone knows that."

"Well, what he actually said, or should have said," continued Mr. Rummage, "was "one small step for 'a' man, one giant leap for mankind". But the 'a' wasn't heard because of a transmission blank. At least that's what NASA said. Later, Neil sort of admitted that he might have forgotten it—that he'd blown the line he'd rehearsed over and over again!"

"But the landing was a huge success, wasn't it?" said Hannah. "He got that right."

"He certainly did," declared Mr. Rummage, "and that's what really counts."

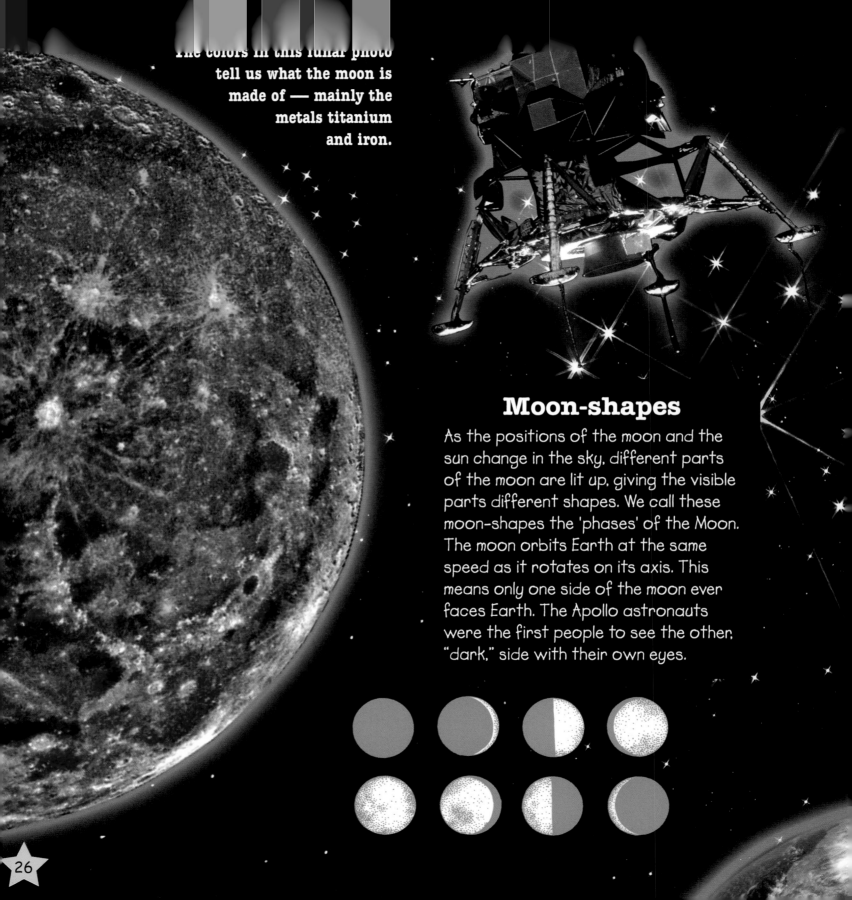

The colors in this lunar photo tell us what the moon is made of — mainly the metals titanium and iron.

Moon-shapes

As the positions of the moon and the sun change in the sky, different parts of the moon are lit up, giving the visible parts different shapes. We call these moon-shapes the 'phases' of the Moon. The moon orbits Earth at the same speed as it rotates on its axis. This means only one side of the moon ever faces Earth. The Apollo astronauts were the first people to see the other, "dark," side with their own eyes.

LUNAR DATA

Earth's satellite

The moon orbits Earth and is the brightest object that can be seen in the sky. But the moon doesn't create its own light. Instead, it shines by reflecting light from the sun. If the sun were a giant light bulb, the moon would be like a mirror reflecting light from the bulb.

Moon facts

Age: about 4.5 billion Earth years
Diameter: 2,160 miles (3,476) kms
Distance from Earth: 238,857 miles (384,403 kms)
Orbits the Earth in: 27 days, 7 hrs, 43 mins
Rotates on its axis: 27 days, 7 hrs, 43 mins
Hottest temperature: 253°F (123 C°)
Coldest temperature: -387°F (-233 C°)
Day and night: 24 Earth days long

"I don't think I'd want to go to the Moon. Weird things can happen," said Digby, with a shiver.

"Oh? What kind of things?" asked Mr. Rummage, with a twinkle in his eye.

"Well, I've heard you shouldn't stare at the full moon or you'll go mad. And what about all those witches flying around on broomsticks and people turning into horrible werewolves?"

"That's silly," said Hannah. "People make stuff up just to scare little kids like you."

"Hannah's right, Digby. But it probably did feel a bit spooky to be standing on the moon. Just imagine what it'd be like to gaze up at all those stars in the black sky."

"I bet you'd feel pretty lonely," said Hannah, "I'm not sure I'd like to be looking out at millions and millions of miles of nothingness."

A SILENT WORLD

The lunar landscape is made up of mountains, valleys, and plains, pockmarked by craters. The surface is rocky and covered in a layer of dust. There's no wind on the moon, so the footprints made by Neil Armstrong and other astronauts will stay where they are for centuries to come.

Neil Armstrong left an olive branch on the moon's surface as a wish for peace for all mankind.

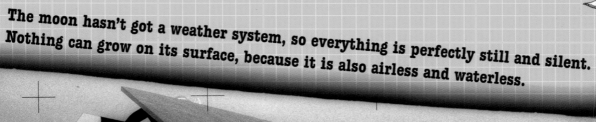

The moon hasn't got a weather system, so everything is perfectly still and silent. Nothing can grow on its surface, because it is also airless and waterless.

27

Moonscapes

The dark regions on the moon are called "maria." They are smooth, flat plains with few craters. The lunar mountains, or "highlands," are made up of huge numbers of overlapping craters ranging from 3.3 feet (1 m) to 621 miles (1000 km) across. The craters were formed long ago by meteorites crashing into the moon's surface.

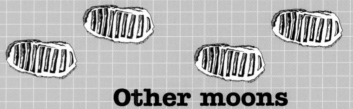

Moon rocks

Between 1969 and 1972, Apollo missions brought 842 pounds (382 kg) of moon rocks, pebbles, sand, and dust back to Earth. Moon rocks teach us about the early history of the moon, our solar system and our own Earth. Moon rock experiments suggest the moon was formed by debris created when a planetary body the size of Mars struck the Earth billions of years ago. In fact, the youngest moon rocks are as old as the oldest Earth rocks—between 3 and 5 billion years old .

The moon rock that Digby found.

Other moons

All the other planets in our solar system have moons except Mercury and Venus. Jupiter has 16 moons, Saturn has 18, Uranus has 15, Neptune has eight, and Mars two.

29

LUNAR SCIENCE

Once they landed, the Apollo astronauts carried out a number of experiments. These included monitoring moonquakes and measuring distances between lunar landmarks. They also recorded changes in the way the Earth rotates and identified the gases in solar wind.

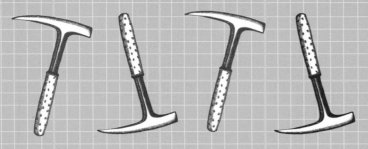

Moon shoot

Photos of the moon's surface and its landscape have allowed scientists to draw maps of it. In fact, there are some areas on Earth that haven't been mapped as accurately as the moon. That's because there aren't any clouds, mists, or trees on the moon to hide the details.

Still working

Although no one has been to the moon for some time, the instruments put there by astronauts are still working to detect moonquakes and meteorite impacts. They continue to measure the movement of the moon and what it is made of. Instruments are also measuring heat and radioactivity below the surface.

"I bet there wasn't much to do on the moon," said Digby.

"Oh but there was," said Mr. Rummage. "And one of the most important jobs was to collect moon rocks."

"Why would anyone want those?" asked Hannah impatiently.

"For learning all about the moon—how long it's been there, what it's made of, and a lot of other fascinating stuff—that's what," replied Mr. Rummage.

"And we've got a moon rock of our very own," said Digby. "I'll add it to my collection if that's all right, Mr. Rummage."

"Certainly, Digby," said Mr. Rummage with a smile.

"So what happened after all the rock collecting?" asked Hannah, who was getting impatient.

"Well, Neil and Buzz uncovered a plaque mounted on the platform of the lunar module. It was read out to a TV audience of millions who were glued to their sets—"Here men from the planet Earth first set foot on the moon, July 1969 A.D. We come in peace for all mankind."

"Wow!" breathed Digby." "I wish I'd been there."

"Me too," agreed Hannah.

"After that," continued Mr. Rummage, "they raised the American flag and talked to President Richard Nixon on a radio-telephone. Then they climbed back into the lunar module and closed the hatch. It was time to go home."

"I bet they were looking forward to getting home," said Hannah.

"I'm sure they were," said Rummage, "but they probably weren't looking forward to the shock of hitting the Earth's atmosphere and splashdown."

"How fast were they going, Mr. Rummage?" asked Digby.

"About 25,000 miles per hour (40,230 km)."

Hannah looked scared, "But shouldn't they have been slowing down?" she asked.

"No, the module had to go fast enough to make sure it entered Earth's atmosphere rather than bouncing off it. Of course, if they'd got it wrong, that's what might have happened."

"Scary thought," shuddered Digby.

"Everything had to work just right. After all, they risked being hurled out into space or burned to a crisp in Earth's atmosphere. It must have been a real white-knuckle ride! The crew waited as the parachutes took a long time to fill. But at last they did, and the module splashed down into the Pacific Ocean."

"Great!" said Hannah, "So they finally got to see their families."

"Oh no," said Rummage shaking his head. "As soon as they got out they were put into quarantine!"

"You mean like sick cats and dogs?" said Digby, looking horrified. "That was a cruel thing to do."

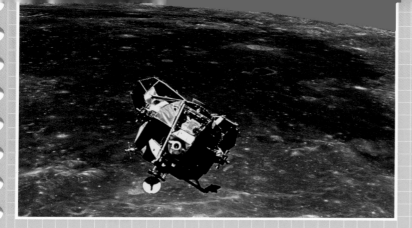

The Eagle leaves the moon and speeds back to the command module. It's time to go home.

In quarantine

The astronauts were flown to the waiting ship by helicopter. They stayed in a sealed quarantine unit. Experts kept a close eye on them to see if they'd been physically or mentally affected by their journey into space. Luckily all of the crew members were in good health and the goals of the Apollo expedition had been met. Mission Accomplished!

SPLASHDOWN

On July 24, 12:15 p.m. EDT, the Apollo 11 capsule splashed down in the Pacific Ocean. The crew had to get used to Earth's gravity and the movement of the module in water, which probably made them feel queasy. But when the recovery ship arrived on the scene, a flotation collar was fitted around the module to hold it steady and the men were helped out.

The Apollo 11 space capsule in a flotation collar.

"I'm so glad I found this rock, Mr. Rummage," said Digby. "I'll put it in a special glass case so people can see it."

"Thanks, Mr. Rummage," said Hannah as they got ready to go home. "He'll probably charge people to look at it."

"Oh no I won't, said Digby.

"I bet you will," countered Hannah.

"I won't"

"You will…"

"Oh, Digby, can I look at your rock? Can I hold it for a second?" asked Pixie, who ran up behind the bickering children.

"Yes, sure," said Digby, handing over his new prize possession.

"Oh, I can feel warmth in it," said Pixie, closing her eyes. "There's definitely energy in here. I can feel it in my fingertips!"

"Mmm," said Digby. "You feel it Hannah, it's quite warm."

"It's been sitting in the sun, of course it's warm, silly," snorted Hannah.

"Shh! It's probably connecting with other moon rocks," sighed Pixie.

"It came back from the moon in a bag. It's a piece of rock. It doesn't do or feel anything," said Hannah, giggling. "Sorry Pixie, we have to go. Come on Digby.
Bye, Mr. Rummage.
See you next week."

AMERICA CELEBRATES

After his work in space, Neil Armstrong held the position of Deputy Association Administrator for Aeronautics, NASA Headquarters of Advanced Research and Technology, from 1970 to 1971. He resigned from NASA in 1971 and was honored with many awards.

On their return, Armstrong and his crew were driven through the streets of Washington in a ticker-tape celebration.

THE APOLLO SUCCESS STORY

Some people wonder why the Apollo missions were carried out at all. They believe that the billions of dollars spent on space travel could have been better spent elsewhere. But the program contributed a lot to space research and rocket development. It landed 12 men on the Moon between 1969 and 1972—although no astronaut has traveled outside Earth's orbit since, due to the high cost. Nevertheless, the space program has benefited from the experience gained through Apollo.

The Apollo 11's success story extends beyond the moon. It has fueled the exploration of other planets and has contributed to our understanding of the histories of Mercury and Mars. Since then, space probes have been flown to the outer planets of our solar system:—Jupiter, Saturn, Uranus, and Neptune. And exciting information has been sent back to Earth on two new rings around Uranus and Neptune's Great Dark Spot. Who knows where space travel will take us next!

GLOSSARY

hover To remain floating, suspended, or fluttering in the air

lunar Referring to, involving, or caused by the moon

mannequin A life-size full or partial representation of the human body; a dummy

Mission Control A ground-based group of people who control and monitor space missions

module A part of a spacecraft that performs a specific task or group of tasks that make the craft work

NASA National Aeronautics and Space Administration

orbit The path of a space body or object as it revolves around another body or object

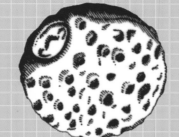

INDEX

Other characters in the Stories of Great People series.

KENZO the barber has a wig or hairpiece for every occasion, and is always happy to put his scissors to use!

YOUSSEF has traveled to many places around the world. He carries a bag full of souvenirs from his exciting journeys.

SAFFRON sells pots and pans, herbs, spices, oils, soaps, and dyes from her spice kitchen stall.

Mrs. BILGE pushes her dustcart around the market, picking up litter. Trouble is, she's always throwing away the objects on Mr. Rummage's stall.

Mr. CLUMPMUGGER has an amazing collection of ancient maps, dusty books, and old newspapers in his rare prints stall.

JAKE is Digby's friend. He's got a lively imagination and is always up to mischief.

COLONEL KARBUNCLE sells military uniforms, medals, flags, swords, helmets, cannon balls—all from the trunk of his old jeep.

CHRISSY's vintage clothing stall has all the costumes Digby and Hannah need to act out the characters in *Mr. Rummage*'s stories.

BUZZ is a street vendor with all the gossip. He sells treats from a tray that's strapped around his neck.

PRU is a dreamer and Hannah's best friend. She likes to visit the market with Digby and Hannah, especially when makeup and dressing up is involved.

Mr. POLLOCK's toy stall is filled with string puppets, rocking horses, model planes, wooden animals—and he makes them all himself!